Framework
for Creating a Great
FINANCIAL PLAN

Now you can create a
Great Financial Plan
for yourself

Lim Cher Hong, ChFC®

PARTRIDGE
A Penguin Random House Company

ISBN: Softcover   978-1-4828-2368-4
             eBook   978-1-4828-2369-1

To order additional copies of this book, contact
Toll Free 800 101 2657 (Singapore)
Toll Free 1 800 81 7340 (Malaysia)
orders.singapore@partridgepublishing.com

www.partridgepublishing.com/singapore

"*Framework for creating a Great Financial Plan* is a starting point to achieve great financial success."

Lim Cher Hong, ChFC® has also co-authored the book "Transform" together with Brian Tracy and other leading authors.

I dedicate this book to three women in my life. One is none other than my wife, Kai-Ling, who has taught me about the importance of frugality. Another is my mum who has sacrificed all her life to raise me up to who I am right now. Finally, my sister who has given me her utmost support.

Contents

Introduction

As I write this book, the world is continually changing. Information that we know now will be obsolete within days, hours, minutes, or even seconds. We need to find an evergreen framework for us to innovate. In earlier days, no one actually understood the meaning of financial planning. All they knew was that they had to save in order to survive. This principle still has its place in the modern world. However, as we progress, our economy has grown to be very complex. Our reliance on professionals like financial advisors and/or bankers to provide financial advice increases.

Sadly, even after engaging a professional, sometimes we may not be able to meet our financial objectives or goals. Our financial portfolios were very affected by the economic downturn, as well as advisors giving us conflicting advice or even wrong advice. These problems were sometimes compounded by advisors changing jobs and leaving us stranded. No offence to any financial advisor out there, because I am guilty myself. I am one of those advisors who changes jobs very often from one bank to another for career progression and/or other career aspirations.

To prevent over-reliance on advisors or bankers, you need to master the art of constructing a good financial plan for yourself. If you are an advisor or banker, it is all the more necessary for you to read this book as your client is going to be filled with vast knowledge when they get hold of this book. This book will instruct them on the essence of a great financial plan which they can create for themselves. As you step your foot into the future, you need to arm yourself with the most relevant information to better plan for your client. This book will provide you with the framework to create a great financial plan.

You can hardly find any books that teach you how to create a financial plan for yourself. There are many books out there that write about financial planning, but they are mainly written for financial advisors. Almost none really writes about financial planning for yourself. Those which have been written on personal finance are mainly focused on money management. However, there are other aspects such as risk management, which is either not touched on, or vaguely covered. Perhaps the only reason why it is not covered is because financial planning requires professional training and certification which is not easy for a layman to understand. This framework to create a great financial plan book is not used to replace any financial planning books out there, nor does it promise to do away with any professionals. In fact, in almost every chapter, I will highlight the type of professional which is required for your financial planning success.

This book only provides you with the *framework* of a financial plan. You will not find advance investment strategies or complicated tools to help you plan. All you need to have is a basic understanding of simple personal finance. Even if you do not have the knowledge, I will be providing a link to my website to further illustrate my message. Financial planning is not always about using the most advanced tools to plan. What is more important is to understand the concept behind the planning. Rule of thumb, *do not invest your time and money in things which you do not understand.* By keeping things simple, you will be able to meet your financial goals and/or objectives. I have seen many successful stories about people who simply just focused on one or two instruments with which they were familiar and they were able to achieve great financial success. You can be like them if you follow my framework.

It's a myth to think that financial planning is only for the wealthy. Everyone needs to plan for their finances. Even if you are heavily in debt, worry no more. This book will guide you on how to get out of the burden of your debt. And if you are already rich, congrats. This book will guide you on how to protect your wealth and grow it further. I have personally used some of the strategies in this book for myself and have achieved great financial success.

I wasn't born with a silver spoon in my mouth. When I was young, I used to stay in a small one-room rented flat with my mother and sister. My mum had to work long hours to support the family. Life was very tough for her, so I made a decision to study hard and hopefully get a well-paid job when I grow up and give my mum a better life. I decided to go into the banking and insurance industry to provide wealth management advice as I fully appreciate and understand the importance of financial planning. When I was working in banks and insurance, I realized that I was merely selling what the company wanted me to sell even though they kept emphasizing to sell based on customer needs. There was something missing, so I decided to pursue a professional qualification and so gained a "Chartered Financial Consultant" title.

Now, you do not have to be like me and pursue a professional qualification to create a great financial plan. You can do it as well. All you have to do is to follow through the framework in this book to create a plan for yourself. You do not need to read from cover to cover if you already have a plan in place or you just want to start planning on one or two particular areas, just flip to the relevant chapter to read. However, you are strongly encouraged to read from cover to cover as you may learn some useful new concepts which you may not have heard of, or you may find it a good refresher. At the end of the book I have also included a sample of a Financial Plan. You can treat it like a template for your own financial plan. However, do take note that, if you are planning together with your spouse, or planning for your business, there may be other aspects which you need to consider which may not be covered in this book. You are strongly advised to seek a qualified consultant such as a chartered financial consultant or chartered financial planner to help you plan. Before you commit to any plan recommended, do confer with more than one consultant from different companies for better comparison.

In chapter one, I will be sharing with you the changes and new approaches in financial planning. In chapter two, I will be introducing you to my four-steps framework and 8 key areas of a great financial plan. From chapter three to fourteen, I will be going through the four steps and 8 key areas in greater detail.

Chapter One

"Money can't buy happiness, but neither can poverty."
—Leo Rosten

C urrently, when we talk about financial planning, we will attribute this to the job of a financial advisor or wealth manager from the bank. However, as the world is changing, people like yourself are getting more educated. You will not merely follow the advice from your advisors; instead, you are likely to be more critical and not always agreeable to their advice.

Although, without a framework of a financial plan, your decision-making process will just be based on your own intuition and experience. This is rather risky. What you feel or think may not equate with reality. Your very own experience may not be adequate or up to date with the current state of the economy. You may miss the boat when opportunity arises or worse, get into an investment plan which is not in line with your risks and objectives.

Very often, I hear my customers telling me" Hey, Cher Hong, I'm so happy I met you. Do you know I have met so many advisors trying to provide me with some form of advice. However, none of them actually went into detail about creating a financial plan for me like you did. All they did was introduce some new product for me to buy. Sometimes when I would buy from them, I began to regret it after I went home. I didn't know what I had bought or why I had bought it in the first place." Does this sound familiar to you, too?

Clearly, to avoid all these pitfalls, you need to know how to create a financial plan for yourself. With a financial plan on hand, you will be able to ascertain whether the advisor's advice is in line with your risk appetite and/or objectives. Your decision process becomes much easier and more definite.

In this new world, *the person who wins is the one who has a great financial plan on hand.* Without a financial plan, you are at the mercy of the advisor providing the advice. But *with* a financial plan, you will be able to know your current financial situation and find the right solution to overcome any shortfall. You get to review your own financial plan almost anytime through your life.

Now, how did I actually come up with this framework? I simply worked with different frameworks used by banks and insurers for their advisors and changed it to be more relevant to you. As for the 8 key areas of a financial plan which I will be introducing to you, it was taught in my Chartered Financial Consultant course. I have taken away the pain from you by synthesizing all these bits of information to make it simple for you to understand. You do not require any special knowledge to grasp what is written in this book.

Chapter Two

"Money is power, and you ought to be reasonably ambitious to have it.

—Russel H. Conwell

Earlier in the introduction, I mentioned that I wasn't born with a silver spoon in my mouth. I was eleven when I was staying in the small one-room rented flat with my mother and sister. My mum had to work long hours to support the family. Likewise, my sister had to pay tuition to support her own studies. Life was very tough for us

As for me, being young, I wasn't able to find a job. All I could do was be thrifty and save as much of my weekly pocket money as possible. Weekly, I was given 50 dollars from my mum. That was a big sum to me at that period of time. However, if I did not know how to save, by the third or fourth day, I would probably have spent everything. Why do I say that? At that time, I was studying in a well-known school where most of the students came from well-to-do families. Everything that they brought to school was simply the best and the latest. Be it school bags, stationary, books, comics, etc, they always had something new to show off.

To be honest, at that earlier stage I couldn't resist the temptation. I started buying things which I didn't really need, but it made me feel good owning them as all my peers had them. So by mid-week, I had spent all my money. I didn't dare tell my mum, so I struggled to live with it. I didn't change my habit immediately. It took me almost a month before I realized that what I had done was wrong.

I started listing down all the things that I had bought for the past weeks and classified them into needs and wants. From the needs, I further identified whether there was a cheaper option. As for all my wants, I resisted getting any of them. However, I tried another way to acquire my wants for free. Free? Yes, for free. Whenever I saw my friends buying new things, I would go up to them and check whether they still needed their old stuff (which were still relatively new). Most of time, they didn't need them. So I simply asked them whether they would give them to me. Most of the time, they would give them to me. If it was something which I didn't want, I would try to resell it to someone else who wanted it. For those that were not willing to part with their old stuff, I would try to buy from them at a much lower price and resell it to another at a higher price. To my surprise, my weekly 50 dollars or more was still in my wallet. I enjoyed the outcome and process which I replicated year after year.

I graduated as a top business student when I was pursuing my degree and I went into banking to provide wealth management advisory. While working in banking and insurance, I achieved many awards and gained recognition both locally and internationally throughout my working career. However, after working for a few banks, I realized that most of the time I was merely selling products which the company wanted me to sell even though they kept emphasizing for me to sell based on customer needs. It occurred to me that financial planning is like having a product and creating a need out of it. Consciously, that was not right. There was something missing, so I decided to pursue a professional qualification Chartered Financial Consultant to understand more about the process of creating a great financial plan for all my clients.

I started reading a lot of books on financial planning and wealth management, some of which were very detailed. However, some concepts were very difficult to understand if you had never studied finance and economics before. I did a lot of research on the financial planning process from various banks and insurers. I then used their frameworks and changed them to be more relevant to you. As for the 8 key areas of a financial plan which I will be introducing to you, it was taught in my Chartered Financial Consultant course. I have taken away the pain from you in order to synthesize all these bits of information and make it simple for you to understand. You do not need any special knowledge to grasp what is written in this book. However, you do need to have basic knowledge of how to calculate the time value of money using a financial calculator, excel spreadsheet, or mobile apps.

I personally used the same framework for myself and achieved great success in my financial life for my whole family. It helped me to uncover my areas of shortfall. I started to analyze each problem and worked out a solution to resolve it. Even though I'm a financial planner myself, the journey was not without struggle. At the beginning, I couldn't come to terms with my current financial situation. I didn't realize that I was very far from reaching my financial goals. I wanted to give up, but I realized that, if nothing was done, I might be worse off, and never get a chance to meet my financial goals. I implemented some solutions on areas which I thought were more important to me, and I set a dateline for myself on other areas that I needed to work on in the future. Whenever there were changes in my financial situation I reviewed my own financial plan. If there were no changes, then every three months I would check to see whether my plans were in line to achieve my financial objectives. Every little change brought me closer to my financial goals.

Chapter Three

"Wealth is not his that has it, but his that enjoys it.
—Benjamin Franklin

Most of the examples and concepts in this book will be based on a Singapore context, but they are applicable to international practices as well.

Now this is all you have been waiting for. The framework of a great financial plan.

Below are **the four steps of the framework**:

1) Preliminary assessment of your financial needs and goals.
2) Developing a Financial Plan
3) Implementation
4) Monitoring and reviewing

In Step 2 of the Financial plan, we will be covering **the 8 key areas**:

1) Money Management
2) Credit Management
3) Risk Management & Insurance Planning
4) Education Planning
5) Retirement Planning
6) Investment Planning
7) Tax Planning
8) Estate Planning

The most difficult part of financial planning is simply to start constructing the plan. If you are serious about planning, go and get a pen and paper now to start constructing. Alternatively, you can get a laptop or a smart phone and start typing. In the next few chapters, I will be going through details of the respective framework. This is where the work begins.

Remember you need to take action in order to achieve financial success. *By not taking any action, you are certainly not going to change your financial situation.* I hope this book will serve you and help you achieve financial success through having a great financial plan for yourself.

Chapter Four

"Academic qualifications are important and so is financial education. They're both important and schools are forgetting one of them."

—Robert Kiyosaki

Knowing and analysing your current financial situation

T o begin writing your own financial plan, you need to conduct a preliminary assessment of your current financial situation.

1) Age

Your age plays a very important part in your financial plan. The earlier you start to plan, the earlier you meet your financial goals. It's never too early to start planning.

If you are studying right now, you can consider what I did when I was young. However, you need to be prepared to receive some setbacks. You may not be able to resell your friend's items that easily. If you are planning to resell, do consider using different channels such as your own direct selling, online marketing, social media etc to sell. Parents may complain if they find out you are selling their children's items, or when you are selling things to their children. Make sure your school does not have any rules against selling products before you start selling.

If you need to support your own education, you need to know the years to your final graduation. In chapter 10, I will be going through with you in detail how to plan for your education.

<u>What is your current life stage?</u>

- Are you planning to get married? If you are, when would it be?
- or Are you planning to have your first child, second or more? If you are, when would it be?
- Are you planning to get a house or planning to get another house for investment? When would it be?
- What are you saving up for, and when do you need it?
- How many more years to desired retirement age?

If you are already at your retirement age, I sincerely hope you have already saved up enough to enjoy your retirement years. If not, do consider getting a full time or part time job if you are medically fit. The challenge here is you may not get the job that you like to do, or a salary may not meet your expectation.

2) Marital status

If you are single, you need to know whether you are planning to get married. If you are, when would it be? You need to save up for your marriage. Your financial situation is going to change. You need to take into consideration your potential spouse's financial situation.

If you are not planning to get married, it is important for you to seriously plan for adversity such as disabilities and long term care. Who is going to take care of you in times of adversity?

3) Employment status

If you are currently unemployed, when are you going to work? Do you expect yourself to find one anytime soon? If not, do consider looking for a temporary or part time job to supplement your life style.

If you are employed, are you planning to change a job anytime soon? If you are out of job or being retrenched, will you be able to find a job soon? Is your pay enough to sustain your life style?

If you are self-employed, do you have any income when you are not working?

4) Income

Do you have any income right now? If not, are you doing anything about it?

Is your current income able to sustain your current life style? If not, do you want to consider changing another job?

Any possibility to create another stream of income or even better create multiple stream of passive income?

5) Dependents

List down the people, businesses or associations that are financially dependent on you? What happens if you are not able to provide for them?

6) Any additional information

- Any hazardous hobbies, smoking habit, etc
- Any likely changes in personal, financial and family situation in the next 12 months.

Risk Profile

There are basically 6 types of risk.

1) Risk Adverse
   Investor who avoids risks and does not mind lower returns to preserve capital
2) Conservative
   Investor who seeks to preserve value by investing into low risk securities
3) Moderately conservative
   Investor who requires a stable income and expects small fluctuations in value to gain modest capital growth
4) Balanced
   Investor who desires a reasonable stable income stream, but also desires a steady growth in capital value and is prepared for fluctuations in the medium term
5) Moderately aggressive
   Investor who is willing to accept fluctuations in capital value for capital growth and does not need the capital in the mid-term
6) Aggressive
   Investor who is willing to take a higher risk for the potential of capital growth and does not need the capital for the long term. Is prepared to invest bigger amounts during market down turns

Below is the sample questionnaire to ascertain your risk profile if you have no idea which category you fall under:

1) What is your risk tolerance?
   a. I am seeking 100% capital preservation   (0)
   b. I am seeking very low risk investment   (1)
   c. I am willing to accept occasional losses
       as long as money is in sound investment   (2)

    d. I am willing to accept fair amount of investment risk to achieve long-term capital growth (3)

    e. I am willing to take higher investment risk to achieve good potential return (4)

    f. I am willing to take on a large amount of risk in order to achieve high capital growth (5)

2) How would you describe your level of investment experience?
   a) I have no experience in investment. (0)
   b) I have little investment experience. (1)
   c) I have some investment experience (2)
   d) I have investment experience (3)
   e) I have board investment experience (4)
   f) I am very experience in investment (5)

3) In the event of a negative investment climate, how easy can you meet your unforeseen financial needs without liquidating your current investments?
   a) Impossible (0)
   b) Very difficult (1)
   c) Difficult (2)
   d) Should be able to (3)
   e) easily (4)
   f) very easy (5)

4) How would the short-term investment decline affect you emotionally?
   a) Drastically (0)
   b) Greatly (1)
   c) Directly (2)
   d) Moderately (3)
   e) Minimally (4)
   f) No effect (5)

5) Which hypothetical investment portfolio would you prefer?

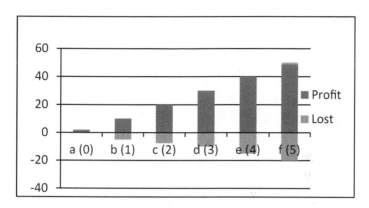

Add up the total score and tally your result with the table below to ascertain your risk profile:

Score	Risk Profile
0	Risk Adverse
1-5	Conservative
6-10	Moderately Conservative
11-15	Balanced
16-20	Moderately aggressive
21-25	Aggressive

By understanding your own risk profile, it will better help you to decide how you going to plan for your investments.

Financial Goals and Concerns

After conducting your preliminary assessment, you need to identify your financial goals and concerns for your **family, yourself, your business, and any other concerns which you may have.**

If you do not know what sort of goals and concerns you have, below are typical financial goals and concerns for you to choose from:

1) Income for loved ones in the event of premature death
2) Income for self and loved ones in the event of a disability
3) Funds for emergency needs
4) Funds for a specific goal at a planned date
5) Funds for children's education
6) Funds for retirement
7) Funds to pay off debt
8) Wealth preservation and distribution
9) Business continuity in the event of your death

Make sure your goals and concerns are specific, measurable, achievable, relevant, and time-bound (SMART Goals). It should be quantified in today's dollar.

Rank your financial goals and concerns in term of importance and wants. Alternatively, you can rank it according to short term, medium term or long term.

Chapter Five

"Let our advance worrying become advance thinking and planning."

—Winston Churchill

Developing a Financial Plan

A great financial plan consists of 8 key areas.
Namely: Money management, credit management, risk management, & insurance planning, education planning, investment planning, tax planning, and finally, estate planning.

Information from one area may be used in another area. For example, in money management, cash flow and net worth statement information will be used in risk management & insurance planning.

Some areas may not be relevant to you. For example you do not need education planning if you do not plan to have a child.

During the whole planning process you will be making some assumptions to facilitate your calculations. Note that any changes to the assumptions may have drastic results. You are strongly advised to compare the results whenever you make changes to the assumptions.

Below are some assumptions which you should consider right now:

Personal Assumptions

1) Life expectancy
   You should check with your statutory board on the statistic for life expectancy for male and female. However you should also consider your family history. How old were your great grand parents or grandparents when they passed on (if they already passed on)? If you are too lazy to find out, for females you can use 85 and for males 83. Yes, all statistics prove that women live longer than men.

2) Desired retirement age
   As life expectancy increases every year, retirement age likewise is higher. Each and every country has its own retirement age set. However, you can choose to retire as early as you want. Consideration is whether you have enough to last throughout your life time. Problems arise when you outlive your savings.

3) Projected salary increase per year

4) Projected increase in expenses per year

5) University entry age for children & number of years to provide for university education (if any)

6) Whether you will be retiring together with your spouse (if any)

7) Whether group insurance (if any) is taken into your calculation

Economic Assumptions

1) Savings interest rate per year
2) Fixed deposit interest rate per year
3) inflation rate per year
4) Current investment rate of return
5) Post retirement rate of return
6 Increase in university education costs per year

Above are just some of the examples. You may uncover more assumptions as you plan along.

Do not get carried away when you plan. Make sure you refer back to your financial goals and objectives regularly. You need to know your own affordability, tax position, and risk tolerance. Always work on your most important goals first. The 80-20 rule applies here. You should be using 80% of your effort—to plan for top 20% of your financial goals.

Chapter Six

*"A good idea is about ten percent and implementation
and hard work, and luck is 90 percent."*

—Guy Kawasaki

Implementation

Implementation is by far the most important part of the whole financial plan. Imagine you have the greatest plan in the world, but you choose to sit on it; your life will still be the same, and nothing can be changed.

In the earlier chapter, we mentioned that you have to prioritize your financial goals. After prioritizing, you must set timelines to achieve your financial goals.

This is where you need to consult a professional like a Chartered Financial Consultant to help you evaluate your own financial plan, a lawyer to help draft or vet through your Will, a tax officer to further check on any other claimable amount or deductable, and a regular doctor who has your medical history, also, banker to advise you on investment or loans, etc. Do keep their contact in your phone book or mobile phone for easy reach.

After seeking the advice from all the professionals, it is important that you make your own decision whether to take their advice or seek a second opinion. Before you take any action, make sure you are fully aware of the features and benefits of the product. What are the risks inherent in the product? As well as the commitment period and whether it is the best comparing to other similar products. Best does not necessarily mean the cheapest. What is more important is whether the product is able to meet your financial goals and objectives.

Monitoring

Do not assume that all your plans will definitely meet your financial goals. It is important to schedule time for reviewing. Recommended time frame is every 3 months. If you are reviewing with your advisor or banker, please do not act on their advice immediately. More often than not, they may be eager to get another sale from you. Do evaluate your options properly. Ironically, sometime doing nothing may be the best solution. Just make sure you are on track with what you have already planned.

You should also review your financial plan whenever there are changes in your financial situation. For example, you may be getting married, planning to have a child, planning to buy a house or you may be out of job and unlikely to find a new job anytime soon, etc. You have to decide what sort of changes to be made to your plan. Do you have to get another product or liquidate any investment, etc?

Chapter Seven

"Money Management has been a profession involving a lot of fakery - people saying they can beat the market, and they really can't."

—Robert J. Shiller

Money Management

In this chapter, we will be looking at cash flow and net worth statement. You may be saying, "Wait, Cher Hong, I do not have any accounting background. I won't be able to understand." Don't worry, I will be going through with you how to create the cash flow and net worth statements as well as help you to understand how to read the statement.

The objective of creating a cash flow and net worth statement is to understand your current cash flow and your current net worth. It will give you an overview of your current financial situation. I will also briefly go through how you can manage your credit.

Cash flow Statement

First, list down all your cash inflow. Below are some example of possible cash inflow:

1) Gross Salary and wages, or self-employed income
2) Commissions
3) Bonuses
4) Allowance
5) Annuity payment
6) interests and dividends
7) Rental income
8) Proceed from liquidation of assets
9) Any other sources of income

Next list down all the cash outflows. There are basically two types of cash outflows.

1) Fixed
   This recurring cash flows which occurs month after month, year after year

2) variable
   This amount tends to be different every time. You need to exercise control over the occurrence. For calculation purposes, find the average over a period of time or simply give an approximation.

Below are examples of fixed outflows

1) rental payments
2) mortgage payments
3) other loan repayments (e.g. car loan, renovation loan, etc)
4) insurance premium payments
5) regular savings
6) parent's or children allowance
7) child's school fee

Below are examples of variable outflows

1) food and clothing
2) personal expenses
3) children's expenses
4) household, utilities and other related costs
5) holidays expenses
6) medical and dental cost
7) transportation or car maintenance
8) taxes.

Note: variable components can be fixed in your situation and vice versa. For example food, you may be ordering from daily meals which can be considered a fixed amount. Mortgage payments can be different every month depending on the current interest rate environment.

Template for a Cash-Flow Statement

		$	$
1)	**Cash Inflow**		
	Your list	x	
	Total inflows (Add up all your inflows)	xx	**XXX**
2)	**Cash Outflow**		
a)	Fixed outflows		
	your list	y1	
	Sub- total (Add up your fixed outflows)	yy1	
b)	Variable outflows		
	your list	y2	

Sub-total (Add up your variable inflows)	yy2	
Total outflows (Add up your fixed and variable sub-total)		**YYY**
Net Cash Flow (Surplus/Deficits) (=1-2)		**ZZZ**

Note: Above input is annualised. If you have the monthly amount, you simply multiply it by 12 to get the annual figure.
Three possible outcomes when total expenditure is deducted from the total income:

1) a cash surplus (income > expenditure)
2) a zero balance (income=expenditure)
3) a cash deficit (income < expenditure)

If the outcome of the net cash flow is surplus/positive, it means that you have excess cash for your planning. However if you have deficit/negative net cash flow, it does not necessarily mean you are doomed. What is important is that you must understand what are the contributing factors for the deficit. Be aware of the weaknesses and strengths of the current cash position. This will be further illustrated when we do budgeting next.

Budgeting

This is where we study in the detail each item of the cash inflow and cash outflow.
Create another cash flow statement for the purposes of budgeting.
For cash inflow, you need to find out whether there are ways to improve the amount. For example whether you can create another

income stream for yourself. Whether you can get higher interest from another bank for your deposits. Don't assume all banks are paying the same interest. Or instead of a savings account, can you put into a time/fixed deposit to generate a higher interest.

For cash outflow, you need to find out whether there are ways to reduce the amount. Based on the above examples of the fixed and variable cash outflows, below are the ways to reduce the amount:

Budgeting for fixed outflows

1) mortgage payments
   Find out whether you are able to do re-pricing within the same bank or refinance to another bank.

2) other loan repayments (e.g. car loan, renovation loan, etc)
   Find out whether you can reduce the interest rate for example by reducing the tenor. Using other forms of loans for the same purpose. For example a term loan for revolving credit.

3) insurance premium payments
   Find out whether there are other cheaper premiums option for the same type of plan.

4) regular savings
   Again, find out the higher interest regular savings accounts, or investing in a mutual fund, etc.

5) parent's or children's allowance
   This would be a sensitive area to reduce. It will be taken care of when the savings above are done.

6) child's school fee
   Find out whether there is a grant, scholarship, or sibling discount.

Below are examples of variable outflows

1) food and clothing
   Visit restaurants less often, go to coffee shops, instead of Starbucks, go to tailors instead of buying brand-name clothes. This is another sensitive area where you are required to change your lifestyle. These are just my suggestion, but if you follow them, you are likely to save tons of money.

2) personal expenses
   Find out whether you are able to reduce any personal expenses such as "wants" which you can go without.

3) children's expenses
   This is usually the area where parents spend the most. I can write a whole book on this topic. This is another sensitive area where values are inculcated. I do not wish to elaborate here, but you be the judge of what is more important for your child.

4) household, utilities, and other related costs
   This is another big topic to discuss here. The gist of the matter is to find the cheapest form without compromising the quality. Save, save and save more.

5) holiday expenses
   Cut down the number of travels, or go to neighboring countries instead. Compare the cheapest package

6) medical and dental costs
   Any reimbursement from company of employment, government-linked medical center or free clinic.

7) transportation or car maintenance
   Take public transport instead of driving or vice versa. Find out whether there are any concessionary rates.

8) taxes.

Minimize tax payable, maximise deductions and reliefs. Will discuss more in chapter 13

Now, compare the two tables above and see how much savings you have. I'm sure you are amazed by the amount you can save here. I understand you have taken great pains to come this far, and I really hope you have made an effort to come up with the actual numbers and not just any hypothetical numbers.

Next we will be preparing our net worth statement.

Net Worth Statement

Net worth = Assets - Liabilities

Robert T. Kiyosaki mentioned that Assets are anything that puts money into your pocket and liabilities are anything that takes away your money.

So how do we value an asset?

An asset is measured either at fair market value, or the actual value of the assets, or the price that the asset can reasonably be expected to sell for in the open market.

There are basically 3 types of assets:

1) Cash/Near Cash Assets - low risk liquid assets which are either cash or easily convertible into cash. For example, savings accounts, time deposit accounts, current accounts, cash value of insurance plans etc

2) Invested Assets - acquired in order to earn a return. For examples, stock portfolio, unit trusts, investment properties, business ownership, government savings, etc

3) Personal Use Assets - For examples. place of residence, cars and other vehicles, personal property such as jewelry, etc

And we have 2 types of liabilities:

1) Current liabilities - due for full payment within 1 year from the date of net worth statement. For examples, outstanding balance on credit cards, short-term loans outstanding, bank overdraft, or credit line, etc

2) Long Term Liabilities - due for full payment 1 year *or more* from the date of net worth statement. For examples, home mortgage balance outstanding, long term loans outstanding e.g. car loan, etc

Net Worth Statement Template

Assets	S$	$Liabilities	S$
Cash/ Cash Equivalent	AA	Current Liabilities	EE
Investment Assets	BB	Long Term Liabilities	FF
Personal Use Assets	CC		
Total Assets	**DDD**	**Total Liabilities**	**GGG**
		Net Worth (Total Assets - Total Liabilities)	**HHH**
		Total Liabilities + Net Worth	**DDD**

The outcome of the net worth position is either positive or negative. If the outcome is positive, it simply means that, if you liquidate all your assets, it will be able to cover all your liabilities. If the outcome is negative, you ought to be worried. You need to

27

work extra hard to generate more assets and pay off your liabilities as much as possible in the shortest period of time.

Find out whether you require insurance protection for your assets and liabilities. Also find out whether you need to diversify your investments. All these will be covered in greater detail in the next few chapters.

Below are the common 8 **Financial Ratios** used in the Money Management planning:

1) **Basic Liquidity Ratio**
   = Cash/ Near Cash
   Monthly Expenses

Measures the ability to cover expenses using cash/near cash in an emergency situation.
Guideline: 3 to 6 months

2) **Liquidity Assets to Net Worth**
   = Cash/ Near Cash
   Net Worth

Indicates what % of net worth should be in cash or cash equivalents.
Guideline: minimum 15 %

3) **Savings Ratio =   Savings**
   Gross Income

Indicates % of gross income to set aside for future consumption.
Guideline: greater than 10% is good

4) **Debt to Asset Ratio =   Total Debts**
   Total Assets

Measures liquidity or the ability to pay debts
Guideline: less than 50% is good

5) **Solvency Ratio =** <u>**Net Worth**</u>
Total Assets

Measures potential longer-term solvency problem
Guideline: greater than 50% is considered healthy

6) **Debt Service Ratio**
= <u>Total Annual Loan Repayments</u>
Total Net Income

Measures the level of debt compare to take home income.
Guideline: Less than 35% indicate sufficient take home pay to service debt.

7) **Non-Mortgage Debt Service Ratio**
= <u>Total Annual Non-mortgage Loan Repayment</u>
Total Net Income

Measure debt level as well, but excludes mortgage payments
Guideline: Less than 15% is considered safe.

8) **Net Investment Assets To Net Worth Ratio**
= <u>Total Invested Assets</u>
Net Worth

Measure the level of capital accumulation
Guideline: greater than 50% is considered healthy.

If you have difficulties in constructing the cash flow statement, net worth statement, budgeting or financial ratios, do engage a freelance accountant to help you construct. A good financial planner will be able to help you as well.

Chapter Eight

"The idea that somebody is going to come in and make your debt go away and all be well for the future is really a fantasy."

—Victoria Moran

Credit Management

The objective of credit management is either to eliminate debt totally, or to reduce the amount of debt. Risk of debt could be financed through insurance contracts.

When you borrow to finance present consumption, it is a form of credit or debt. There are basically two type of credit.

1) revolving (open ended)
   Line of credit, overdraft, credit card, etc

2) Long term (Closed ended)
   Mortgages, car loans, renovation loans, unsecured personal loans, etc.

Below is the process for credit management:

1) List down all debts and liabilities in order of the highest interest to lowest rate of interest.

2) Find out whether there are any ways to reduce the interest or start paying off loans with the highest interest first. For example, ask for re-pricing of your mortgage with your current financer or re-finance it with another financer. Check whether there is another type of loan which can serve the same purpose. For example, using a mortgage term loan for your personal loan if the total interest and cost is lower.

3) Identify if you have any large expenditures such as buying a house in the foreseeable future. Provision needs to be made.

4) Consider using credit protection insurance or mortgage reducing term insurance to manage your credit risk. (More will be discussed in the next chapter.)

Ensure that you maintain a good credit bureau record. Pay your loans promptly. Do not apply for too many loans or credit cards at the same time. Stagger your applications if you have to. It is a myth to think that if you do not have any credit history, you will be able to get a loan easily when you need it. On the contrary, loans are not easily approved if there is no credit history as a company does not have any record to ascertain the risk.

Check with various banks and finance companies on their loans or credit products for better comparison.

Chapter Nine

"Risk comes from not knowing what you're doing."
—Warren Buffet

Risk Management & Insurance Planning

T he objectives of Risk Management are to identify the risk exposures and adopt alternative methods to deal with risk. Not all risks are insurable. However, many potential serious events can be insured against by transferring them through insurance contracts to insurers.

Business Risk Management

If you are running your own business, you need to analyze your business risk. Find out if there is a better way for your business set up. For example, if you are a sole-proprietor or in a partnership, you may want to consider changing it into a private limited or limited liabilities company instead. Ensure that you have a business succession plan in place. Adopt credit protection insurance or golden handcuff to retain your staff if applicable. Examples of golden handcuffs are long service awards or pension funds for your loyal staff.

For business risk management, you should seek insurance agents who are specialised on business risk management for advice.

Life Insurance Planning

Ensure that you provide adequate funds for the living needs of your loved ones in the event of premature death, partial or total permanent disability, critical illness, hospitalization (medical expenses), long term care, education needs, outstanding debts payoff, taxes, etc.

Below is the process for Life Insurance planning for premature death:

1) Calculate total existing life insurance coverage available. Complications can arise when your company offers an employee insurance scheme, do you take that into consideration.

   The risk to be taking into consideration is that group benefits can be changed by an employer, benefits may changed or ceased when you change employer, or benefits may be ceased at certain age.

   Another consideration is when you have a personal accident insurance, again do take that as a consideration. The risk is that personal accident only covers for death as a result of an accident and the policy is yearly renewable and premiums are not guaranteed. For prudent calculation, we will not take group insurance and personal accident insurance into consideration.

2) Calculate the total assets available which can be extracted from the net worth statement. It will be prudent to remove all non-liquid assets such as properties and cars out of the equation.

3) Sum up the total existing life insurance coverage and the total assets available.

4) Calculate the total amount of liabilities/debts outstanding which can be extracted from the net worth statement.

5) Find out your last expenses for your funeral. (As long as this is not a taboo subject for you.)

6) Calculate the amount needed to provide for your children's education needs. (Refer to chapter 10 for education planning calculation.)

7) Calculate the total amount needed to provide until your last dependent is no longer around. Assuming that your spouse is not working, and his or her current age is 35 and is expected to pass on at age 85, he or she still has 50 years to go. On the assumption that he or she is not able to find a job after you pass on, you still have to set aside provision for his or her daily expenses.

8) Shortfall/surplus for premature death
= [(4) + (5) + (6)+ (7)] - (3)

Positive means there is shortfall and vice versa.

Below are some common individual life insurance contracts to meet this shortfall:

1) Term insurance: Provides protection for specified period. If death occurs during this period, the face value of the policy is paid, with nothing being paid in the event that the insured survives the period.

2) Whole Life Insurance: Provides protection for the entire life. Premiums may be paid throughout the insured's lifetime, over a limited period, such as 10, 20, or 30 years, or to a specified age. The premium may also be paid in one lump sum at the inception of the policy, in which case the policy is referred to as a single-premium whole life policy.

For Life Insurance planning for total & permanent disabilities, we need to add additional cost such as nursing home fee to the shortfall for premature death. Note that disability can also be partial or temporary. In both cases, you may still be able to work but may be earning a lower income. For prudent calculation, we would want to consider the worst scenario that is total and permanent disability. Total & permanent disabilities coverage is normally embedded into the basic policy. If it is not included, chances there is an option to include it as a rider.

To calculate Critical Illness requirement, you take your annual income multiply by 2. You can get a standalone critical illness plan which covers early stage critical illness. Alternately, you can add a critical illness rider which normally only covers terminal stage critical illness.

For Hospitalization & Medical expenses, you should get a comprehensive insurance plan based on your affordability and needs.

For long term care, it is required when one is in a state of coma where life-sustaining measures are put in place. It is advisable to consider having an advance medical directive to object to any life-sustaining measures if it is allowed in your country. You can also have long term care insurance plan if it is available.

For Life insurance planning, you can seek a professional Chartered Financial Consultant or Chartered Financial Planner to help you plan.

Non-Life insurance Planning:

There are 3 main types of non-life insurance planning:

1) Providing protection against loss or damage to property such as house, home content, car, etc - Fire insurance, home content insurance, motor insurance respectively.
2) Providing indemnity against third party claims- This can be in the form of riders for the above insurance plan in point 1.
3) Providing coverage for your overseas trips. It could be in the form of a single trip travel insurance or annual plan travel insurance if you travel very often during the year.

Note: Your current health condition, occupation, hobbies, lifestyle, etc, will affect your insurance planning. Your insurance application may be rejected or additional premiums may be loaded. Also, if you have children, when they grow up and start working, you may not need the coverage anymore.

Most of the non-life insurance plans will be able to be purchased online. If you have doubts, contact the insurer directly.

Chapter Ten

"Formal education will make you a living; self-education will make you a fortune."

—Jim Rohn

Education Planning

I f you have children, this will be one of your main priorities to plan and plan early. Education costs are high and generally rising faster than the rate of inflation.

Below are the calculation steps to determine the amount needed for children's education:

1) Determine the current cost of tertiary education for one year, taking into consideration the place of study and the desired course fee including living costs.
2) Calculate the total current costs to provide for the required number of years.
3) Compute the future cost of the total current cost of education. Taking into account the assumption for the educational inflationary rates.
4) List down the current assets/investments you have set aside for this need.
5) Shortfall or surplus for education = (3) - (4)

6) Determine the current amount needed to save per year from now till the start of the course.

The above method could be used to plan for other lump sum savings needs such as businesses, buying a new house, etc. The only difference may be that you do not have to calculate the required number of years to provide for, and you do not have to calculate the inflationary rates.

Any financial planner or banker will be able to help you plan for your children's educational needs.

Chapter Eleven

"Preparation for old age should begin not later than one's teens. A life which is empty of purpose until 65 will not suddenly become filled on retirement."
—Dwight L. Moody

Retirement Planning

The objective is to have enough funding for the rest of your life when you retire from your job.

There are 2 methods of calculating retirement needs:

1) Replacement ratio method - Determine the desired income at retirement needed at today's value.
2) Expense ratio method - Using the current expense to determine the amount needed for retirement.

For prudent calculation, you may want to determine your current expenses and then add a factor of 20-30% to calculate the desired income. I call it Expense-replacement ratio method.

Replacement ratio method calculation steps:

1) Decide the retirement income you need at today's value.
2) Determine the number of years to retirement (= Age intend to retire minus current age)
3) Determine the future value of required yearly income at retirement taking into account the inflationary rates assumption. This is also the first year retirement income needed at retirement.(PMT)
4) Calculate the number of years to provide (=death age - retirement age)
5) Calculate the lump sum needed to fund the retirement needs from retirement till death by taking into account the inflation-adjusted investment rate of return*(PV)
6) Identify the available sources of income to fund the retirement. Possible sources of retirement income such as any government provident fund, supplementary retirement scheme, bank deposits, rental income, investment, endowment insurance policies, annuities, inheritance, etc.
7) Shortfall or surplus for retirement needs = (5)-(6)

* [(1+investment rate of return)/(1+inflation rate) - 1] x 100%

Expense ratio method

Similar to replacement ratio method calculation steps, instead of desired retirement income, we use current annual expenses instead.

Any financial planner will be able to help you on retirement planning. However, the method of calculation may vary from above.

Chapter Twelve

"Part of being a winner is knowing when enough is enough. Sometimes you have to give up the fight and walk away, and move on to something that' more productive."

—Donald Trump

Investment Planning

The basic objective of most people is to earn the maximum possible after-tax rate of return on the funds available for investment, in line with the level of risk taken. This is referred to risk-return trade-off i.e. the greater the potential return, the higher the potential risk, vice versa is true as well.

There are basically 2 types of risk:

1) Systematic Risk/ Market Risk: Risk that is not diversifiable. Example, interest rate risk, exchange rate risk, purchasing power risk, tax risk, etc.
2) Unsystematic Risk/ firm-specific risks: Risk that is diversifiable. Example, Financial/credit risk, business risk, liquidity and marketability risks, investment manager risk, etc.

There are predominantly four investment styles:

1) **Value investor** one who relies on fundamental analysis of a company's financial performance to identify stocks priced below intrinsic value.

2) **Growth investor** one who seeks companies that promise to boost intrinsic value rapidly.

3) **Technical investor** one who uses mathematical indicators and chart to look for imbalances in supply and demand.

4) **Portfolio investor** those who ascertain their investment risks and assemble a diversified securities portfolio bearing that risk level.

For simplicity, we will be using portfolio investor theory for investment planning process.

Below is the investment planning process:

1) Analyze your current financial situation. List all your investable assets. Find out the historical return of the assets. Find out the weighted-average rate of return on all the assets. (=Sum of all the returns/ total number of assets)

2) Identify your financial goals and objectives for investment. Is it for income or capital gain? Desired rate of return.

3) Know your risk profile and set an investment time horizon

4) Your investment knowledge, preference, and experiences.

5) Ensure you have sufficient emergency funds before investing.

6) Identify any weakness in the current asset mix such as over-concentration of certain assets. Redeem some if necessary, and diversify into other assets.

7) List the new assets mix and find out the expected rate of return and its weighted-average rate of return. Check if it is in line with your desired rate of return; if not, try changing the assets mix or reduce your desired rate of return.

Below are the common investment products:

1) **Cash**: refers to current assets comprising of currency or currency equivalents that can be accessed immediately or near immediately such as savings, fixed deposits, money market funds, etc.

2) **Fixed Income**: refers to any type of investment under which the borrower/ issuer is obliged to make payments of fixed amounts on a fixed schedule. for example, borrower has to pay interest at a fixed rate once a year, and to repay principal amount on maturity such as bonds.

3) **Stock**: refers to the equity stake of its owners. It represents the residual assets of the company that would be due to stockholders after discharge of all senior claims such as secured and unsecured debt.

4) **Currency**: refers to money in any form when in actual use or circulation, as a medium of exchange, especially circulating paper money.

5) **insurance products**:

6) **Unit Trusts**: a form of collective investment scheme under a trust deed.

7) **Hedge Funds**: refers to a pooled investment vehicle administered by professional management firms that employ leverage and invest in a diverse range of markets and use a wide variety of investment styles and financial instruments.

8) **Real Estate Investment Trusts**: refers to a company that owns, and in most cases operates income-producing real estate.

9) **Real Estate**: refers to investment in property for profit through rental and/or sales.

10) **Exchange Traded Funds**: refers to an investment traded on stock exchange, most of which tracks an index.

11) **Commodities**: refers to a class of goods for which there is demand, but which is supplied without qualitative differentiation across a market.

12) **Futures/Options/Warrants**: refers to a form of derivatives

13) **Equity/ currency-linked products**: refers to the product return that is linked to the underlying equity/currency without having directly invested into it.

Entering an investment is a difficult decision but getting out is even harder. Always set your take profit and cut loss level and stick to it. Do not rush into reinvesting your money. Make sure it is in line with your investment risk and objective.

Different assets classes have different levels of risk. Below is the ranking from the lowest to highest risk. (From left to right)

Being a risk adverse investor does not mean that you can only invest in cash. In fact, you should still have equity and/or currency in your portfolio. The difference is the percentage allocation to equity and/or currency which should be lower compared to cash and/or fixed income. Likewise for an aggressive investor, the only difference is higher percentage placed on equity and/ or currency and other alternative investment assets such as commodities comparing with cash and fixed income.

Unit Trust funds tend to be good investment tools if you do not have or have only limited investment experience. It is managed by a professional fund manager who invests based on a given mandate.

Do seek a wealth manager or personal banker from the bank to provide you with investment advice if you do not have or have only limited experience in investment. Above processes and types of products only serve as a guide. You need to have in-depth knowledge and experience to be successful in investment. There are many investment talks, courses, and books out there. The more you attend or read, the better you are.

Chapter Thirteen

"The hardest thing to understand in the world is the income tax."

—Albert Eintstein

Tax Planning

The objectives of tax planning are minimizing tax payable, and maximising deductions and reliefs. Check with your jurisdiction whether you are able to enjoy any tax exemption. For example if you are self-employed, married with kids, etc. Does your government offer any form of supplementary retirement scheme to enjoy deferment of income tax? You need to understand the advantages and disadvantages of doing so. Any charitable contribution made which will qualify you for deduction

It is advisable to start planning one year ahead to see how you can maximise deductions and reliefs. You will be able to ascertain your earnings based on the last 3 years tax assessment and your own projection for the year ahead.

Assuming you are a Singapore Resident filing tax in Singapore, you can use the income tax calculator for computation for your tax as below (Based on Year of Assessment 2014):

Income:	$
Employment income	0
Less: Employment Expenses	0
Net Income	0
Trade, Business or vocation (Less: **Allowable Expenses)**	0
Add: Other Income	
Dividends	0
Interest	0
rent from property	0
royalty, change, estate/trust income	0
gains or profits of an income nature	0
Total Income	0
Less: Approved Donation	0
Assessable income	0
Less: Personal Reliefs	
Earned income relief	0
Spouse/handicapped spouse relief	0
Qualifying/handicapped child relief	0
working mother's child relief	0
Parents/handicapped parent relief	0
Grandparent caregiver relief	0
Handicapped brother/sister relief	0
CPF/provident fund relief	0
Life insurance relief	0
Course fees relief	0
Foreign Maid Levy relief	0
CPF cash top up relief (self, dependent and medisave account)	0
Supplementary retirement scheme (SRS) relief	0
NSman(Self/Wife/parents) relief	0
Chargeable income	0
Tax Payable on Chargeable Income	0
Net Tax Payable	0

If you are still in doubt, do seek a professional tax officer to advise you on tax matters.

Chapter Fourteen

"Estate Planning is an important and everlasting gift you can give your family. And setting up a smooth inheritance isn't as hard as you might think."

—Suze Orman

Estate Planning

The objectives of estate planning are to find out the provision of liquidity for your personal and dependents' financial needs should anything unfortunate happen during your lifetime, and for your dependents upon your death; making provision for your immediate expenses; and preservation & distribution of wealth and enhancement of wealth.

Estate consists of everything a person owned or jointly owned with someone else which includes both assets and liabilities.

Below are the estate planning checklist:

1) **Will**: A Will is a legally-enforceable declaration of what people want done with their probate property and their instructions about other matters when they die. Ensure that you have a will. Make sure the Will is up-to-date. You may want to consult a lawyer to ensure that your Will is valid.

2) **Nomination for any government provident fund**: Ensure nomination is made according to your preference. If nomination is made before your marriage, you may want to consider making changes if possible.

3) **Existing Insurance**: Ensure nomination made for beneficiary/beneficiaries. Check that it in line with the Will.

4) **Property ownership**: Is the property bought under Joint-Tenancy or Tenancy-in-common? You may want to check with a qualified property agent &/ lawyer on the differences and its implications.

5) **Trust**: A trust is a fiduciary arrangement set up by someone, called the grantor, creator, or settler of the trust, whereby a person, corporation, or organisation, called trustee, has legal title to property placed in the trust by the grantor. People usually use this to avoid probate. More often than not people do not need one.

6) **Estate Duty**: Any overseas assets which require one to pay estate duty. You can consider using insurance to fund it.

7) **Guardianship for children**: This is especially important if you have a minor or special needs child. Do consider appointing a guardian.

8) **Incapacitation**: Any arrangement made such as nursing care? Consider drawing up a lasting power of attorney.

9) **Making gifts**: Consider passing your assets in the form of gifts. Some jurisdiction may have concession for estate duty when assets are passed on as gifts.

You can seek a professional chartered financial consultant or chartered financial planner for your estate planning matters. He or she will be able to further recommend any other professional in your particular circumstances.

Chapter Fifteen

"If all the economists were laid end to end, they'd never reach a conclusion."

—George Bernard Shaw

Conclusion

L et's do a recap of the framework of a great financial plan. There are basically **four steps**:

1) Preliminary assessment of your financial needs and goals.
2) Developing a Financial Plan consisting of 8 key areas:
   i) Money Management
   ii) Credit Management
   iv) Risk Management & Insurance Planning
   v) Education Planning
   vi) Retirement Planning
   vii) Investment Planning
   viii) Tax Planning
   ix) Estate Planning
3) Implementation
4) Monitoring and reviewing

This first thing you must do is get a pen and paper to start constructing. Alternatively, you can get a laptop or a smart phone and start typing. I hope you have already done so even before reading the conclusion.

Let me end this by sharing a story of my client. For confidentiality, he will be known as Mr. Tan. Mr. Tan was referred to me by one of my clients three years back. Mr Tan is a sole breadwinner with three young children living in a four-room flat together with his wife. Two year ago, he was retrenched from his manufacturing company and has been out of a job since then. He ran into financial hardship and had been living on his savings and borrowing from the bank. He was very stressed and went into gambling. His debts snowballed to a level which was beyond his capability to repay and his behavior became very aggressive and easily agitated whenever he went home. This was a challenging case. I did the best I could to help him. I helped him draft out a simple financial plan. For a start we agreed to set his priority on clearing his debt and I went through the credit management with him. I suggested to him ways to reduce his interest as well as making a special arrangement with the banks on the repayment scheme. He was on the verge of being sued by the bank for bankruptcy, but I prevented it from happening with my advice. As he was out of job for almost a year, it was important for him to find one soon. I suggested to him to reduce his expectations and guided him on refining his resume and some interview techniques. He managed to find an outdoor sales job. His base pay was not high but, if he were able to bring in sales, he would be able to earn as much, or even more, than what he was getting from his last job. I gave him some encouragement and taught him some skills in salesmanship to increase his chances of closure. His job also allowed him to send his children to school and pick them after school. I suggested to him that he should allow his wife to go out and work. Eventually he agreed, and now his wife is working as a clerical staff worker. Since his eldest son is already fifteen years old, I assured him that he should entrust his eldest son to look after his two younger siblings. To his surprise, his two other children were also very well-disciplined and helped out with the housework;

they also had completed their homework whenever he and his wife reached home. Once his debt arrangement was settled and family arrangements were taken care of, I guided him to plan for other areas. He showed me his financial plan which I thought was brilliant. He was able to come up with recommendations which I had never taught before. Recently, he shifted into a bigger five-room flat and was leading a comfortable lifestyle, even though he is still paying back his debt which was manageable. I'm very happy for him and, upon some self-reflection, I realized that it was the financial plan which he has created that helped him through the difficult time. This is also where I got my inspiration to write this book on the Framework to create a great financial plan.

Now, regardless of your financial situation, you, too, can be like Mr Tan leading a comfortable lifestyle through a great financial plan. I hope my book has served you by showing you the framework to create a great financial plan. I wish you all the best and may you achieve great financial success in life.

Acknowledgement

I would like to dedicate the completion of this book to the following people. I never thought I would be able to write a book myself if not for the expert advice from Brian Tracy whom I happened to come across when I googled for sales. I was inspired by him that everyone wants to write a book in their lifetime, and I do not need to be a genius to write one. I purchased some of his products and found many useful contents. He also recommended other gurus such as Brendon Burchard and Nick Nanton from whom I also purchased some useful programs. Since then I have read many best-selling books such as *The Secret* by Rhonda Byrne, *Rich Dad Poor Dad* by Robert T. Kiyosaki, *Think and Grow Rich* by Napoleon Hill, *Seven Habits of Highly Effective People* by Steven R. Covey, *The Total Money Makeover* by Dave Ramsey, etc. in the market which broadened my knowledge. Certainly, without my family support, this would not have been possible. One is none other than my wife Kai-Ling who has taught me about the importance of frugality. Another is my mum who has sacrificed all her life to raise me up to become who I am right now. Finally, my sister, who tolerated all my nonsense and gave me her utmost support. Next, I would like to give special thanks to all my clients who have given me their support throughout these years. Some of whom have become very close friends such as Mdm Tjong who has been my client since I started my career. Coincidentally, she was my assigned client when I progressed to another company. Finally, the Chartered Financial Consultant program offered by Singapore College of Insurance has transformed me into a professional consultant providing sound advice for all my clients.

Sample

Profile
Family information:

You & Immediate Family:	Relationship	Date of Birth	Age	Occupation
Mr C Wong (You)	Self	12/12/1976	38	Sole-proprietor (Owner of Printing Shop)
Mdm K Tan	Wife	01/01/1978	36	Accountant
Jackson	Son	06/06/2008	6	Student in childcare (Kindergarten)
Jenny	Daughter	11/11/2010	4	Student in childcare (Pre-Nursery)
Other Family Members:				
Mr C Wong:				
J Wong	Mother	07/07/1946	68	Retiree
Mdm K Tan:				
T Tan	Father	04/04/1954	60	Technician
P Goh	Mother	05/05/1956	58	Home Maker

Assuming you are a sole-proprietor of a printing shop. Currently, you have 2 full-time staff (One of which is your uncle who is drawing a salary) and 1 part-time staff working for you. You are in the shop most of the time. When you are not around, your uncle is fully in charge. Your income from your business is around $5800 per month. You have 3 dependents that is your son Jackson, daughter Jenny and your mother J Wong. You are a smoker and no other hazardous activities. Your wife is accountant of a publishing company. Her basic salary is $3200. Even though her father is still working, she is giving him and her mother an allowance of $600 each. She does not have any hazardous activities but has high blood pressure which require regular medication.

Risk profile questionnaire:

1) What is your risk tolerance?
   a. I am seeking 100% capital
      preservation (0)
   b. I am seeking very low risk
      investment (1)
   c. I am willing to accept occasional losses
      as long as money is in sound investment (2)
   **d. I am willing to accept fair amount of investment
      risk to achieve long-term capital growth (3)**
   e. I am willing to take higher investment risk to achieve
      good potential return (4)
   f. I am willing to take on a large amount of risk in order
      to achieve high capital growth (5)
   Ans: (d)

2) How would you describe your level of investment experience?
   a. I have no experience in investment. (0)
   b. I have little investment experience. (1)
   c. I have some investment experience (2)
   d. I have investment experience (3)
   e. I have board investment experience (4)
   f. I am very experience in investment (5)
   Ans: (b)

3) In the event of a negative investment climate, how easy
   can you meet your unforeseen financial needs without
   liquidating your current investments?
   a. Impossible (0)
   b. Very difficult (1)
   c. Difficult (2)
   d. **Should be able to** **(3)**
   e. easily (4)
   f. very easy (5)
   Ans: (d)

4) How would the short-term investment decline affect you emotionally?
   a. Drastically   (0)
   b. Greatly   (1)
   c. Directly   (2)
   d. Moderately   (3)
   e. Minimally   **(4)**
   f. No effect   (5)
   Ans: (e)

5) Which hypothetical investment portfolio would you prefer?

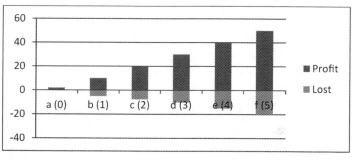

Ans: (e)

Total score: 15   **Risk Profile: Balanced**

Financial Needs and Goals

Family:

1. Income for your three dependents in the event of premature death & events of disability.
2. Funds for Jackson and Jenny local university education.

Personal:

3. Funds for retirement

Business:

4. Intend to leave business to Jackson and Jenny if they intend to carry on running the business

Others:

6) Plan to buy a condominium around $1.5 Million in 3 years time to stay.

Personal Assumptions

1) Life expectancy: You are expected to live till age 83 (taking into consideration lifespan of your parents). Your wife is expected to live till age 85.
2) Desired retirement age: You are expected to retire at age 65 and your wife at age 63. (Retire at the same time)
3) Projected salary increase per year: 0% for yourself (which may be lower due to rising cost) and 3% for your wife.
4) Projected increase in expenses per year: 5% for both of you.
5) University entry age for children & number of years to provide for university education:
    Jackson expected to enter university at age 21 and Jenny at age 19. 3 years to provide each.
6) Whether group insurance taken into calculation: No group insurance for yourself. Your wife has a 100K death and total & permanent disability coverage.

Economic Assumptions

1) Savings interest rate per year: 0.2%p.a.
2) Fixed deposit interest rate per year: 0.6%p.a.
3) Share dividend per year: 4%p.a.
4) inflation rate per year: 3% p.a.

5) Current investment rate of return: 6%p.a.
6) Post retirement rate of return: 6%p.a.
7) Increase in university education costs per year: 6%p.a.

Money Management:

Your Cash Flow Statement

1) Cash Inflow:	
a) Self-employed income	$69,600
b) interests	$220
c) Dividends	$800
Total inflows	**$70,620**
2) Cash Outflow:	
a) Fixed Outflows	
mortgage payments	$12,000
Car loan repayment	$12,000
insurance premium payment	$6,000
parent's allowance	$12,000
child's school fee	$14,400
Sub-Total	$56,400
b) variable outflows	
food and clothing	$7000
personal expenses	$2400
holidays expenses	$5000
transport & car maintenance	$5000
taxes.	$2000
Sub-Total	$21,400
Total Outflow	**$77,800**
Net Cash Flow (Surplus/Deficits) (=1-2) (Deficits)	**-$7,180**

Budgeting

	Before	After
1) All Income:		
Self-employed income	$69,600	$104,400
(Setting up another printing shop in another location or offering franchise, assuming 50% return of current return or earning 50% loyalty fee.)		
interests	$220	$220
(Assuming interest is the best comparing all banks.)		
Dividends	$800	$800
2) All Expenses		
Mortgage Payments	$12,000	$10,800
(Assuming it is already out of the penalty period and you refinance it with another bank with lower interest and instalment reduces to $900 per month instead of $1,000 per month.)		
Car Loan repayment	$12,000	$12,000
(Assuming there is marginal difference in interest rates.)		
insurance premium payments	$6,000	$6,000
(Amount will change when you buy more insurance to cover your shortfall in your financial plan.)		
parent's Allowance	$12,000	$12,000
(This may be a sensitive area to reduce.)		
child's school fee	$14,400	$14,400
(Your children has settled down, not advisable to make too many changes.)		
food and clothing	$7,000	$6,500

(Go to restaurant dining once a week instead of twice a week. Go to food court or coffee shop instead.)		
personal expenses	$2,400	$2,400
holidays expenses	$5,000	$2,500
(Visit neighbouring country such as resort in Thailand, Indonesia or Malaysia.)		
transport & car maintenance	$5,000	$5,000
(Assuming car is necessary for fetching children.)		
taxes.	$2,000	$3,000
(This has increased as self-employed income has increased. However, you may want to consider changing your business into private limited. There may be tax incentives for first year set up depending on your jurisdiction and company tax is separated from personal tax.)		
3)Subtract (2) from (1)	**-$7,810**	**$30,820**

Even though there are deficits initially, with detailed budgeting you can achieve great surplus as highlighted above.

Your Net Worth Statement:

Net Worth Statement December 2013

Assets:	S$
1) Cash/Cash Equivalent	
Savings	50,000
Fixed Deposit	20,000
Cash value of insurance plans	30,000
Sub-Total	100,000

2) Investment Assets	
Government Provident Fund	100,000
Supplementary retirement Scheme	38,250
Blue Chip Shares	50,000
Sub-Total	188,250
3) Personal Use Assets	
Car	120,000
House	600,000
Sub-Total	720,000
Total Assets	**1,008,250**
Liabilities:	
1) Current Liabilities	
Credit Cards	1,200
Income Tax	2,000
Sub-Total	3,200
2) Long Term Liabilities	
Housing Loan	135,000
Vehicle Loan	83,000
Sub-Total	218,000
Total Liabilities	**221,200**
Total Liabilities + Net Worth	**1,008,250**

Financial Ratio:

1) **Basic Liquidity Ratio**
    = **Cash/ Near Cash**
      Monthly Expenses
    = **100,000** = **15.42 months**
      77,800/12

Able to cover expenses using cash/near cash in an emergency situation for about 15 months
Guideline: 3 to 6 months
Able to use 6-9 months of cash/near cash for other purpose.

2) **Liquidity Assets to Net Worth**
    = **Cash/ Near Cash** = **100,000** = **12.7%**
      Net Worth   **787,050**

This is not a healthy level.
Guideline: minimum 15 %
You should find ways to sell off or change some of your investment or personal assets to free up the cash. In this example, it will be more appropriate to change a second hand car of lower value. For government provident funds and supplementary retirement scheme, you will not be able to free up the cash. Since blue chip shares is drawing a consistent good dividend of 4%, you may not want to sell it unless the valuation is too high. As for house, unless it is appropriate to downsize.

3) **Savings Ratio**
    = **_____Savings_____**
      Gross Income
    = **50,000+20,000** = **99.12%**
      70,620

Able to set aside 99.12 % of gross income for future consumption.
Guideline: greater than 10% is good.

This further highlight you will be able to set aside more funds for your financial plan.

4) **Debt to Asset Ratio**
   = $\frac{\text{Total Debts}}{\text{Total Assets}} = \frac{221,200}{1,008,250}$ =21.94%

Able to pay debts using all available assets.
Guideline: less than 50% is good.
Note that some of the assets are not able to be liquidated for the purpose of paying debt. Also during emergency, you may not be able to fetch a good price or ill-liquid.

5) **Solvency Ratio**
   = $\frac{\text{Net Worth}}{\text{Total Assets}}$
   = $\frac{787,050}{1,008,250}$ = 78.06%

Do not have longer-term solvency problem.
Guideline: greater than 50% is considered healthy

6) **Debt Service Ratio**
   = $\frac{\text{Total Annual Loan Repayments}}{\text{Total Net Income}}$
   = $\frac{1,200+2,000+12,000+12,000}{70,620}$
   = $\frac{27,200}{70,620}$ = 38.52%

This is not a healthy level
Guideline: Less than 35% indicate sufficient take home pay to service debt.
You are required to find ways to increase your income as well as reducing the total annual loan repayment.

Note that we are assuming net income is the same as gross income in this case.

7) **Non-Mortgage Debt Service Ratio**
$$= \frac{\text{Total Annual Non-mortgage Loan Repayment}}{\text{Total Net Income}}$$
$$= \frac{1,200+2,000+12,000}{70,620} = 21.52\%$$

This is not a healthy level.
Guideline: Less than 15% is considered safe.
This further highlight you are required to find ways to increase your income as well as reducing your loan repayment.

8) **Net Investment Assets To Net Worth**
$$\textbf{Ratio} = \frac{\text{Total Invested Assets}}{\text{Net Worth}} = \frac{188,250}{787,050} = 23.92\%$$

This is not a healthy level.
Guideline: greater than 50% is considered healthy.
You need to invest more to increase your capital accumulation.

Credit/Debt Management

List down all debts and liabilities in order of the highest interest to lowest rate of interest.

1) Credit Card at 24% p.a. - You should pay off all the credit card bills as the amount is not huge and interest is the highest interest.
2) Income Tax at 20% - You are advised to use all the tax deductible and relief which is applicable to you. You are advised to check with the income tax authorities or tax officer for more advice.

3) Vehicle loan at 1.88% p.a. - You should pay off part of the loan if possible.

4) Housing loan at 1.2% p.a. - Check with your existing financier whether you are able to do a re-pricing to a lower interest package or refinance it with another bank.

You intend to buy a condominium around $1.5 million for investment in 3 years time. You should start saving for it now and pay off the existing housing loan to avoid high down payment and/or having to pay a higher instalment. Alternatively, you may consider a cash out, if interest is not high from the existing property and subject to bank's approval and regulation at that time.

You should consider buying a mortgage reducing term insurance to protect the loan. Get a car insurance if you have not done so.

Risk Management

You should come up with an agreement and make known to all your staff on the taking over of the business in case of mishap happening to you. Without an agreement, your staff may think that your uncle will be taking over the business when you are not around. Consideration should be made as to who will be the interim boss when your children are not yet of legal age to take over the business. Is it your uncle? or your wife?

Consider changing your business into a private limited company instead. This is to ensure continuity of your business, potential tax savings, and limited liabilities.

Adopt credit protection insurance if your business has any liabilities.

Consider offering long service awards or pension funds for your loyal staff.

You should create a joint financial plan together with your wife.

Life Insurance Planning

Total you have 3 endowment policy, $30,000 death and Total & permanent disabilities coverage each for yourself, Jackson and Jenny. Premium $200 per month for yourself and $150 each for both your child. Current market value is $10,000 each.

Do not have any company insurance coverage.

Do not have any personal accident insurance.
Therefore total existing life insurance coverage is $30,000.

Total assets available less non-liquid
= $1,008,250 -$720,000 = $288,250

Total existing life insurance coverage and the total assets less Non-liquid assets
= 30,000 + 288,250 = $318,250

Total amount of liabilities/debts outstanding
= $221,200

Assuming last expenses for your funeral = $20,000

Children education needs:

Number of years to provide for Jackson
= 21-6 = 15 years (n)

Assuming tuition fee is $12,740.52 and living cost is $19,000, total cost = $26,650 (PV)

Education inflation rate = 6% (i)

Estimated total future cost, FV = $76,068 (Using End Mode)

Less: Available education plan = 76,068 - 30,000 =$46,068

Assuming Jenny total future cost is the same, total education needs
= 46,068 x 2 = $92,136

Amount needed to provide for your mother
= $12,000(PMT)

Assuming your mother pass on age is 85, number of years to
provide = 85 - 68 = 17 (n)
Investment rate of return = 6% (i)

Amount required to provide for your mother(PV)
= $133,270.74 (Using End Mode)

Shortfall/surplus for premature death
=221,200 + 20,000 + 92,136 + 133,270.74 - 318,250
= $148,356.74 (Shortfall)

Assuming nursing home fee
= $36,000 per year (PMT),

inflation rate 3%(i),

number of years to provide = 85 - 38 = 47(n),

total nursing fee required, PV = $929,916.17 (Begin Mode)

Total & permanent disabilities required
= 148,356.74 + 929,916.17 = $1,078,272.91 (Shortfall)

Based on the premature death and total & permanent disabilities
shortfall, you should consider buying a term insurance and cover
up to the said amount.

Critical Illness required = 70,620 x 2
= $$141,240 (Shortfall)

You can add this as a rider for the above term insurance. For a more comprehensive coverage, you may want to buy a stand-alone policy. For Hospitalization & Medical expenses, you should get a comprehensive hospitalization & Medical insurance plan based on your affordability and needs.

For long term care, you should consider having an advance medical directive to object to any life-sustaining measures if it is allowed in your country, and get a long-term-care-insurance plan if it is available.

Non-Life insurance Planning:

Besides fire insurance which your wife took up with a mortgage loan, you should consider taking up a home content insurance for your house. Get a mortgage reducing term loan to cover the loan in case of mishap.

You already have a comprehensive motor insurance for your car which is also serviced by your wife.

Ensure you buy a travel insurance whenever you go overseas. If you travel very often during the year, you may want to consider taking up an annual plan.

Since you are a smoker, your premium tends to be more expensive. If possible, try to quit smoking; you can achieve great savings, and you will be less prone to serious illness such as cancer.

Education Planning:

As per life insurance planning:
Children education needs:

Number of years to provide for Jackson
= 21-6 = 15 years (n)

Assuming tuition fee is $12,740.52 and living cost is $19,000, total cost = $31,740.52 (PV)

Education inflation rate = 6% (i)

Estimated total future cost, FV = $76,068 (Using End Mode)

Less: Available education plan = 76,068 - 30,000 =$46,068

Assuming Jenny total future cost is the same,
total education needs = 46,068 x 2 = $92,136

Assuming investment rate of return 6%(i),
FV = $92,136 & n=15 years,

amount to save per year = $3,734.36 for both children (Using Begin Mode).

Therefore, each has to save $1,867.18.

Planning for the purchase of condominium in 3 years time

Value of condominium = $1,500,000

Assuming down payment is 50% of the value
= $750,000

And all other cost such as stamp duty, additional buyer stamp duty, legal fee, renovation is 10%
= $150,000.

Total amount required = 750,000 + 150,000
= $900,000

Amount required to save aside each year assuming FV=$900,000, i = 6%, n= 3 year
= $266,697.01 (Using Begin Mode)

Based on the amount, you may need to defer your purchase. You should consider paying off your existing property first, or sell off before considering buying another property.

Down payment may be lower depending on your country regulation. Some countries may not require any down payment but all other costs still need to be paid.

Retirement Planning

Using Expense-replacement ratio method:
Retirement expenses required (PV)= $77,800

Number of years to retirement = 65 -38 = 27 years (n)

Future value of required yearly income at retirement, assuming inflationary rates 3% (i)
= $172,816.28 (Using End Mode)

This is also the first year retirement income needed at retirement.(PMT)

Number of years to provide(N) = 85 - 65 = 20 years

Lump sum needed to fund the retirement needs assuming inflation-adjusted investment rate of return i= [(1+6%)/(1+3%) - 1] x 100% = 2.91%,

PV = $2,668,039.17 (Using Begin Mode)

sources of income available to fund the retirement
= $188,250

Shortfall or surplus for retirement needs
= 2,668,039.17 - 188,250
= $2,479,789.17 (Shortfall)

Get a retirement insurance plan to cover the shortfall. As the amount is huge, you may want to cover up to your affordability.

Investment Planning

Present situation of investable assets:

Assets	Value	Historical Return	
Savings	$50,000	0.2%	$100
Fixed Deposit	$20,000	0.6%	$120
Government Provident Fund	$100,000	4%	$4,000
Supplementary retirement Scheme	$38,250	0.1%	$38.25
Blue Chip Shares	$50,000	7%	$3,500
Total	$258,250		$7,758.25

weighted-average rate of return for all the assets
= 7,758.25/258,250 x 100% = 3%

Your financial goal and objectives for investment is to achieve desired rate of return of 6%p.a.

Risk profile being Balanced and your investment time horizon is up to age 65

Your investment knowledge is limited to only Blue Chip shares, prefer to invest property and experience in endowment insurance.

You have sufficient emergency funding

Weakness in the current asset mix is over-concentration in Blue Chip Shares and Cash.

Consider redeeming some Blue Chip Shares and investing into mid-cap shares for potential further capital appreciation. Consider using some Cash and invest it into fixed income funds. Since you have to defer your property buying plan—you may want to consider investing into REITS instead, by using half of your fixed deposit. Depending on your jurisdiction policy, you can invest into other instruments such as Global Balanced Fund. Again, if you can invest your Supplementary retirement scheme, you may want to invest into Asian Balanced Fund.

Preferred new assets mix:

Assets	Value	Potential Return	
Savings	$20,000	0.2%	$40
Fixed Deposit	$10,000	0.6%	$60
REITS	$10,000	8%	$800
Global Balanced Fund	$100,000	6%	$6,000
Asian Balanced Fund	$38,250	7%	$2,677.50
Fixed Income Fund	$30,000	5%	$1,500
Blue Chip Shares	$25,000	7%	$1,750
Mid Cap Shares	$25,000	9%	$2,250
Total	**$258,250**		**$15,077.50**

weighted-average rate of return for all
assets = 15,077.50/258,250 x 100% = 5.83%

This is within the desired rate of return.

Tax Planning

Assuming you are a Singapore Resident filing tax in Singapore, you can use the <u>income tax calculator</u> for your tax computation. Below is the tax computation after fully utilizing all the deductibles and reliefs:

Income:	$
Employment income	0
Less: Employment Expenses	0
Net Income	0
Trade, Business or vocation (Less: Allowable Expenses)	30,000
Add: Other Income	
Dividends	0
Interest	0
rent from property	0
royalty, change, estate/trust income	0
gains or profits of an income nature	0
Total Income	30,000
Less: Approved Donation	2,000
Assessable income	28,000
Less: Personal Reliefs	
Earned income relief	1,000
Spouse/handicapped spouse relief	0
Qualifying/handicapped child relief	0
working mother's child relief	0
Parents/handicapped parent relief	7,000
Grandparent caregiver relief	3,000
Handicapped brother/sister relief	0
CPF/provident fund relief	0
Life insurance relief	1,000

Course fees relief	2,000
Foreign Maid Levy relief	0
CPF cash top up relief (self, dependent and medisave account)	4,000
Supplementary retirement scheme (SRS) relief	12,750
NSman(Self/Wife/parents) relief	3,000
Chargeable income	16,250 (<$20,000)
Tax Payable on Chargeable Income	0
Less: Parenthood Tax Rebate	0
Net Tax Payable	0

A tax savings of $2,000.

Estate Planning

1) You have to start writing a Will.
2) You may want to make nominations for government provident funds according to the following allocation: 30% each for your mother, Jackson and Jenny and 10% for your wife. Less amount for your wife as she is currently working and not dependent on you.
3) You may want to consider making nomination for all your policies according to the above arrangement in line with your Will.
4) Your current property is bought under Joint-Tenancy with your wife. If you meet with mishap, your wife will be the rightful owner to the whole property. If you are not happy with this arrangement, you may want to indicate your preference in the Will with your wife's acknowledgement. (Do seek a legal professional for further advice).
5) You do not need a living trust based on your current situation.
6) Currently, you do not need to pay any estate duty.

7) You should appoint your mother as the guardian for Jackson and Jenny as they are still minor.
8) Get a lasting power of attorney and getting your wife to be the executor.
9) You do not need to make any gift for the time being.

Implementation

Prioritising

1) Clear those with high interest such as credit cards.
2) Risk Management for your business - come up with the agreement.
3) Life insurance & Non- Life insurance - Get a term insurance with critical illness rider, hospital and medical insurance, long term care plan, mortgage-reducing term loan.
4) Get an insurance endowment plan for both your children.
5) Purchase the recommended investment asset mix. For Fixed deposit, you may want to wait till maturity.
6) Start working on the reliefs and deductibles for next year tax savings.
7) Estate planning
8) Get a retirement plan up to your affordability.
9) All other plans listed above such as purchase of property when the budget allows.

Monitoring

Change your financial plan above straight after making the purchase or changes. Review your plan after 3 months and thereafter every 3 months or whenever financial situation changes. Remember to update your Will as well.

About the Author

Lim Cher Hong is a Chartered Financial Consultant® who has been working in the banking and insurance industry for the past 11 years. Recently, he has been named as one of America's Premier Experts® in recognition of his knowledge in financial guidance. He has achieved many awards such as; Million Dollar Round Table, which was attained by only the top 3% of Financial Advisor around the world, Top Performer Aviva Achievers Award, and POSB Top Insurance Team Sales Award. Lim Cher Hong has also received recognition as being titled AXA Top Rookie Advisor, which was featured in Straits Time Life Section. While working at Treasures Onshore as a Relationship Manager, he received the Onshore Award & Royal Gold Award.

Upon graduation at University of London he was acknowledged as the Top Business Graduate and was featured in the Today Papers "The First Degree."

He has also co-authored the book "Transform" together with Brian Tracy and other leading authors.

Log on to: www.limcherhong.com to find out more. You will be able to access to many valuable free resources.

You may **connect** with **Lim Cher Hong** at
https://www.facebook.com/limcherhongchfc
https://www.twitter.com/limcherhongchfc
https://www.linkedin.com/in/limcherhongchfc
Email: limcherhong@limcherhong.com